Blissful Real Estate Investing Book

Build massive wealth applying 15 successful tried and true steps of the most successful real estate millionaires.

Every year people think to themselves, "How can I start building for my future?" Then they start looking around for ways to do that, get overwhelmed, and put it off for another time. Pretty soon 5, 10, or 20 years have gone by and they are no closer to reaching their financial goals than when they first asked themselves that question.

If you are looking at this book, you are considering investing in real estate to build for your future. Are you excited but nervous at the same time about investing in real estate? Are you confused about where to get started? Do you feel uncertain about your ability to invest in real estate because of finances, the market conditions, or not knowing enough?

In the revolutionary Itty Bitty Book, Moneeka Sawyer shows you how to get started in real estate investing or grow your current portfolio.

For example you will learn:

- Where is the best place to find the perfect property?
- How to get financing for that property.
- How to manage that property and tenants in a low stress, blissful way.

Pick up a copy of this powerful book today and learn how to build massive wealth the blissful way. That means building wealth on your own terms, part-time, with very little stress.

Your Amazing
Itty Bitty®
Blissful Real Estate
Investing
Book

*15 Steps to Building Massive Wealth
On Your Terms*

Moneeka Sawyer

Published by Itty Bitty Publishing
A subsidiary of S&P Productions, Inc.

Printed in the United States of America

Itty Bitty Publishing
311 Main Street, Suite D
El Segundo, CA 90245
(310) 640-8885

ISBN: 978-1950326-29-7

This book is dedicated to all of you courageous seekers who are wise enough to know that you can have a life filled with joy, passion, meaning, and WEALTH.

And to my wonderful husband who supported me to find the same.

To find out more about Real Estate Investing visit us at the Itty Bitty Publishing site.

http://www.ittybittypubishing.com

or visit Moneeka at

www.Blissfulinvestor.com

———

Table of Contents

Introduction

Welcome to the exciting world of real estate investing. I have so much to share with you! Before getting started, let me tell you a little bit about myself.

1. I have a personal real estate portfolio that I have built over 20 years. I started with a $10,000 wedding gift and have grown it to over $2,000,000.
2. I have grown my real estate portfolio only working 5-10 hours a MONTH and I can teach you how to do the same. Most other experts teach you how to build yourself a new job. That's not my way and it shouldn't be yours either.
3. I teach strategies that are proven and have consistently worked for decades. They are intuitive and easy to implement.
4. I believe in building a portfolio that will support the joy in your life. So, in addition to covering investing strategies that work I also cover strategies for creating the mindset for success.
5. In order to experience joy in your investing you need to have fun. Most real estate investors just focus on the numbers. The truth is that real estate investing is a people business. If you don't know how to deal with that aspect of the business, you will experience the stress that most investors experience. If you learn to keep the business fun and focus on creating good relationships in your investing business you will build a much more

successful business and experience much less stress.

By the time you finish this book you will:

- Understand what it means to build wealth blissfully and how that applies to you.
- Have a set of goals that will inspire you to take action and achieve sustainable success.
- Have decided on a real estate strategy that is just right for you based on your goals, financial situation, and resources.
- Have the tools to start your real estate investing business now.
- Overcome your fears about investing in real estate.
- Feel confident to start investing in real estate immediately.

Remember things don't need to be complicated to be effective. Once you learn how to use these simple tools, a life of joy and massive wealth will be at your fingertips.

Imagine the Possibilities

- Imagine what your life will be like once you feel confident enough to take charge of it.
- Imagine how much more you will be able to do once you have your financial security taken care of.

In the time it takes you to read this Itty Bitty Book your entire future will be transformed. Enjoy your personal journey to blissful wealth.

Step 1
What Does Bliss Have To Do
With Real Estate Investing?

Bliss? What does that even mean? And what does that have to do with real estate investing?

Warren Buffett, one of the richest men in the world, says **"If you can't control your emotions, you can't control your money."**

If Warren Buffet thinks this is important, don't you think you should too? That is where bliss comes in.

Bliss is:

1. Emotional mastery.
2. Emotional resilience.
3. The understanding that even though you can't always control what happens to you or around you in the world, you can control how you choose to respond.
4. Knowing that your responses determine the outcome of your life.
5. Feeling confident that you can handle anything that happens in your real estate business and in every area of your life.

Focusing on Bliss Will Affect Your Investing By:

- Taking your emotions out of your decisions.
- Making you more confident in your decisions.
- Making you more likely to take action on your decisions.
- Helping you to deal with challenges in an expert way with less stress.

Can you see how this is important? If you focus on creating a blissful mindset the end result will be more joy, more success, and more wealth.

Step 2
Where Are You Headed?
Do You Want To Go There?

Now that you see the value of focusing on bliss to build sustainable wealth, how are you going to get there?

The very first step to building blissful wealth is to take stock of where you are and where you are heading. Here are the things to consider.

1. What are you spending most of your time on right now? You probably work eight hours a day and sleep eight hours a day. Where are you spending the rest of your time?
2. What is it that you want to create in your life? Do you want to retire early? Do you want to take nice vacations? Do you want to be able to put your children through college?
3. When you look at what you are doing in your leisure time is it moving you closer to these goals?
4. If not, are you motivated to make the changes needed to achieve your goals?

Exercise to Change Where You Are Headed:

- Get a notebook designated specifically for the exercises in this book.
- For two weeks write down all the activities that you engage in.
- You don't have to write down the specifics of your activities at work. But do write down what you do during your breaks and lunch.
- Include the hours that you go to bed and wake up.
- Include all the activities you do when you are not working or sleeping. Include your meal times.
- After two weeks evaluate what you wrote down. What patterns do you see? Where are you spending the most time?
- For those places that you are spending most of your time, evaluate whether they are serving your goals. It is absolutely okay to have relaxation time. But are you also wasting a lot of your leisure time just because you're not aware of it?
- Write down the things you can eliminate or spend less time on that would give you some time that you could now spend on working towards your goals. For instance, if you currently watch two hours of TV each night, maybe you could just watch one hour. If you spend four hours on the internet each day, maybe you could bring that down to just two hours.

Great job! Now you have freed up the time you need to build your blissful wealth! Let's move to the next step.

Step 3
The First Step To Building
Wealth Blissfully

Now that you have created the time to reach your goals, let's get moving towards achieving them.

Before you can build a blissful life and sustainable wealth you need to know who you truly are.

1. To do this, spend some time getting clear on your core values. You have an exercise on the next page specifically designed to help you do this.
2. Understand that you won't necessarily get this exactly right the first time you go through this exercise.
3. Pay attention and adjust your list when you notice it isn't feeling right to you.
4. Eventually, you will have a list that is exactly right and you'll be able to make decisions and take action that is beautifully aligned with who you truly are.

If you try to build wealth without knowing your core values, fear and self-doubt will constantly stand in your way and cause you stress. So do this exercise first as your foundation to building blissful wealth.

Exercise to Get Clear on Your Core Values:

- Write down 10 of your top values such as family, financial security, bliss, adventure, relationships, joy, safety, learning, excitement, and personal development. These are just a few. To get more ideas, just go to blissfulinvestorbook.com.
- Ask yourself, "If I could have just one value, what would it be?" Write down the first answer that comes to your mind.
- Next, ask "If I could have just one more, what would it be?"
- Repeat this until you come up with your top 5 values.
- Now, take a look at your life. How are you making your decisions? One of the things that cause a lot of fear for people is that they feel they are out of control. They may also feel that they don't make good enough decisions. It's hard to feel blissful if you feel fear. Much of this has to do with the fact that you are making decisions and taking actions that actually conflict with your core values. The more you do this, the more conflicted your life becomes, the more fear you feel, and the more difficult it is for you to feel bliss.
- Start making decisions and taking actions that are aligned with your core values.

Step 4
Setting Your Inspiring Goals

Any time you start something new you need to have a clear idea of **why** you are doing it. If you don't have a specific WHY for embarking on a project, you will quit when you come up against challenges. And challenges always show up.

To find your big WHY, start by asking:

1. What is the ultimate goal or end result you are looking for by reading this book?
2. What is happening in your life right now that you want to change?
3. How can investing in real estate help you create that change?
4. Why do you want that result?
5. What will you gain from it?
6. Go deep on this. For instance, write down your answer to this question, then ask it again. Write that answer down, and then ask the question again. And then do this one more time. Dig deep. This will lead you to the why that will motivate you when things get rough.

Understanding Your Resources.

Once you understand what your deepest goals and desires are, you need to figure out what resources you have to achieve those goals.

Ask these questions to discover the resources you are able to use towards achieving your goals.

- How long do you have to reach this goal?
- How much time can you commit each day or week to reaching this goal?
- How much money can you use to achieve this goal?
- How do you want to feel on your journey toward this goal?
- Do you currently own your primary residence? Do you happen to have equity in that property or somewhere else that you can use toward reaching your goal?

Now that you know your why and what resources you have to achieve that why, let's decide on a strategy that will be perfect just for you.

Step 5
Picking Your Blissful
Real Estate Strategy

Now let's find the best real estate strategy for you based on your personal values, goals, and resources. Here are the major investing categories you have to pick from:

1. Buy and hold: Purchase a property and rent it out. Depending on what properties you buy you can benefit from appreciation and/or get cash flow. Requires very little time commitment. Requires the money for a down payment.
2. Multi-unit rentals: Purchase a property and rent it out. Depending on what properties you buy you can benefit from some appreciation. The focus here is more on cash flow. Requires some time commitment. Requires the money for a down payment.
3. Primary residence purchase and hold: Buy a home and live in it. When you are ready to move, keep it and rent it out. Requires less money for down payment and very little time. Requires more patience.
4. Fix and flip: You purchase a property that is in bad condition, fix it up, and sell it in less than 12 months. Requires high time commitment and cash.
5. Wholesaling: Get a house in contract and sell the contract. Requires high time commitment, but no cash.

Which Strategy is Right for You?

Now it's time for you to pick a strategy that is right for you. Here are the questions to ask yourself.

- How much time do I have to spend on my real estate investing business?
- How much money do I have to invest in my real estate investing business?
- Am I more interested in appreciation or cash flow?
- How quickly do I need to be able to pull money out of this business?
- Can I get loans to finance my real estate business?
- Do I have a network from which I can get investors in my real estate business?

Based on your answers to these questions, pick a strategy you love.

My Favorite Strategy is Buy and Hold because:

- It's easy to understand and implement.
- You can learn along the way without getting overwhelmed.
- If you make a mistake, you can leverage time to recover.
- It is a strategy that works consistently over and over again.

Step 6
Finding the Money You
Need For a Down Payment

I always recommend that you buy your primary residence before you even consider investing in rental properties. Here is why:

1. If you buy your own home first, you are paying monthly towards owning something as opposed to paying a landlord so that they can own something.
2. There are significant tax benefits to owning a house instead of renting.
3. Buying a primary residence is significantly easier than buying an investment property because your required down payment is much lower.
4. Once you own a primary residence, whether you've paid it off or not, you can leverage it to buy other properties.

If you already own a house, you can go to the next chapter that talks about leveraging your current home to buy investment properties.

Getting a Down Payment for Your Primary Residence

There are two things to consider:

- How to get the actual down payment.
- How to get a loan that doesn't require more of a down payment than you have.

There are many options on how to get into a primary residence, even if you don't have a significant down payment.

- FHA Mortgage: requires 3.5% down.
- VA Mortgages: require 0% down.
- First-time homebuyer loans: can require only 3% down.
- Low down payment loans: can require 5%, 10% or 15% down.
- Piggyback loans: Loans that require 5-10% down and piggyback behind your first mortgage.

Some options to actually get a down payment are:

- 401K and IRA loans.

To get more information on your many options, check out TheMortgagerReports.com.

Step 7
You May Have a Down Payment
Right Under Your Nose

Once you have a primary residence you can leverage it to buy an investment property. Once the value of your home goes up, you take an equity line or loan out on the property. Then use that money as the down payment for your investment property or next primary residence. This is how you can use the equity in your current home as leverage to buy another house.

1. You can use that line/loan as a down payment for your next home and rent out the home you are currently living in. If you do this, you get the benefit of getting financing for a primary residence again.
2. The rules for loans on primary residences are much easier to meet than loans for investment properties.

I know this strategy of waiting for equity to build in your property can be a bit slow but there are ways to speed it up. I know I covered this very quickly here. I cover it in much more detail in my Blissful Investor Masterclass if you want to find out more. You can get details on the Masterclass at www.blissfulinvestorbook.com.

Exercise for Using Equity to Buy Another Property

Find out how much equity is currently in your home. There are three steps to this:

- Call a realtor or go online to find the current market value of your home. I use sites like Zillow and Trulia to get this information.
- Find out what you currently owe on your home.
- Subtract what you owe from the value of your home. This is the equity you currently have in the house.

Figure out how much of a loan you could get on that equity. To do that:

- Take the value of your home and multiply it by .80. This is the total amount of the value of the house for which you can get loans.
- Subtract the amount you owe on your house from that number. This is the amount of money you have available to you in the form of an equity line or loan. This is what you would use as a down payment for another home.

Step 8
Blissful Financing Options

Understand that in home financing the more creative you get, the more expensive it will be. But sometimes it is worth it to pay a little bit more in order to get started with a particular property. Refinancing is always an option later.

1. **Conventional Loan:** Cookie cutter 15 or 30 year loans for 1-4 units. 15 year loan will have a lower rate, but significantly higher payment.
2. **ARM loans:** Loans that stay fixed for a certain amount of time and then become adjustable after that time.
3. **Interest-Only loans:** A loan that has a fixed rate and is interest only for a certain amount of time and then fully amortizes over the remaining loan term.
4. **Low Down Payment Options:** Investment property loans with as little as 10% or 15% down.
5. **Stated Income loans:** Loans for people with unusual income situation, such as lots of tax write-offs, commission income fluctuations, etc.
6. **Low Credit Score loans:** If you have a low credit score, there are loans especially for you.

Exercises for Finding the Right Financing for You

- Figure out how much money you have for a down payment.
- Find out what your credit score is. You can do this by going to each of the credit bureau's sites individually: Experian.com, Transunion.com, Equifax.com.
- Find a mortgage banker or broker who has the kinds of loan products you are looking for. You may have to interview several to find the one who carries the right products for you. Don't give up.
- A loan broker will have access to more kinds of loans than a banker at a bank will have. But you will have to pay a little more in processing fees to use a broker.
- If you get turned away by one banker/broker, try another one.
- Get pre-approved for a loan.
- Once you are in contract to purchase a house, get the loan completed and funded.

Step 9
Finding The Perfect Property For YOU!

There is no such thing as a perfect property. But there is a perfect property for your strategy. Follow a few simple steps to determine whether or not a property is good for you.

1. Speak with a Real Estate agent about which areas he/she recommends buying in and discuss any areas you may be interested in to get feedback. Pick 5 or 10 of them on which to do further research.
2. Drive around in those areas during different times of day and evening and pick your favorite five.
3. Have your realtor start sending you search results for properties in those neighborhoods.
4. Evaluate properties to see what the total monthly cost of holding a property will be.
5. Research on-line what current rents would be for each property to see if rents will cover expenses. My favorite places to look are Zillow.com and Craigslist.com.
6. If the rent will not cover your expenses, determine whether you can or are willing to cover the additional expense each month.
7. Once you have determined that the numbers work for you, start looking at properties to buy.

When You Look at a Property Ask Yourself These Questions:

- Do you enjoy walking into this house?
- Do you feel safe in this neighborhood?
- Would this property be easy for you to maintain?
- Based on the kind of tenant you are trying to attract, would that person enjoy living in this house?

Based on your strategy, you may want to ask different questions. What would those questions be? Write them down. To find a more extensive list of possible ideas go to blissfulinvestorbook.com.

If the property passes all of these standards, make an offer that meets your financial conditions. Never offer more than you can afford to hold over the long-term.

Step 10
Building Your Success Team

Real estate is a people business. The people you have on your team can make you or break you. The following are several people you need on your team immediately.

1. Your mortgage broker or banker. This person will help you find the right financing for your purchases and will tell you how much you can afford.
2. Your real estate agent. This person will help you find the right properties that meet your parameters. They know things about real estate you don't know, and may not even know to ask. They can keep you safe and help your business grow.
3. Your mentor. Don't try to re-invent the wheel. It can be the costliest mistake you can make. Get a mentor who is good at what you are trying to do, and learn from their experience and mistakes. This will save you countless hours of heartache and could easily save you a lot of money in costly mistakes.

Additional People You May Need On Your Team:

- A tax consultant that specializes in real estate. You don't need this immediately, but you will need it when you do actually start investing.
- A real estate attorney. In some areas you will need this person on your team right away.
- A team of service providers to help maintain your houses. You don't need this right away. It's good to build this team because it makes everything easier in the long run.

You can find these team members through several sources. Ask friends for referrals, look people up on Yelp, and ask for referrals on local online business groups/lists. I found those lists through networking with other professionals locally. You can go to Chamber of Commerce mixers or check out their list of recommended vendors. You can also go to local real estate group gatherings listed on Meetup.com.

Step 11
Getting Tenants You'll Love

Your tenants are the single biggest factor in how blissful your real estate business is going to be. Treat your tenants like they are your business partners.

1. Keep them very happy.
2. Always refer to their house as their HOME.
3. Train them how to manage the property. Create a system to train your tenants to take care of the property as if it is their own. Do not rent to tenants who are not interested in doing this.
4. Only rent to people you *trust.*
5. Create a *system* for doing complete background checks on prospective tenants. Always check their employment, rental references, and credit.
6. Hand deliver Holiday or New Year gifts.

Determine Your Dream Tenant.

Who is your dream tenant? If you know who you are trying to attract you can buy properties that this type of person would want to live in. You will want to determine property type, quality and neighborhood based on what kind of tenants you want.

Exercise to Determine Your Dream Tenant:

- Write your wish list for qualities you want to see in your tenant.
- You may not find someone who is a perfect match, but knowing who you want to rent to will make the process much easier.
- Use as much additional paper as you need.
- After you have written down your wish list, think about why these qualities are important to you.
- Based on this new information, refine your wish list. Continue to do this until you are happy with what you have come up with.

We cover this in great detail in the Blissful Investor Masterclass. To find out more go to blissfulinvestorbook.com.

Step 12
Blissful Property Management

One of the biggest reasons people don't get involved in buying investment properties is that they are intimidated by the prospect of having to manage them. There are hundreds of horror stories of tenants trashing a place or something going really wrong with a property and the landlord having to deal with a nightmare.

Property Management Tips:

1. Always consider what kind of tenant you want when you buy a property. Your tenants will determine how well the property is kept up. The right tenant will actually manage the property for you.
2. Determine how nice you want your property to be and stay.
3. Determine how much work you can or would like to put into managing and maintaining your properties.

Setting Up Your Property Management Plan

Once you have answered the preceding questions, you'll have a really good idea of what your true expectations are regarding property management. Now set up a system based on this knowledge.

- Only rent to tenants that can keep the property up to your standards.
- When making an offer to possible tenants, discuss your expectations.
- This is a script for what I say to prospective tenants: "This is going to be your home. I don't want to be intruding on your space and life, so it will be up to you to manage the house as if it's your own. In the beginning, whenever there is a problem, you and I will solve the problem together. After a few times, when you understand the standard I like the house to be kept to, and you are willing to take over the management I will allow you to manage the house on your own terms. Does that sound good to you?"
- If they are not willing to manage the property in the way you would like, keep looking for another tenant.
- If they are excited about this prospect, further clarify the details of how the system will work. (I go into this in great detail in my Blissful Investor Masterclass. Go to blissfulinvestorbook.com to find out more.)

Step 13
A Simple Strategy to Keep It All Blissful

There's no doubt about it. Investing in and managing rental properties can be stressful and it may not feel worth it. But here's the thing. Every single super wealthy person uses real estate as part of their wealth plan. And in truth, it's one of the tools of the very rich that you have access to.

1. Whether you are already wealthy or not, you can buy property.
2. And even better, your government supports you to build wealth in this way.
3. Your banking system supports you so you only have to put in about 20% of your own money, and you get to control an asset that is worth five times what you put in.
4. You also get to benefit from the growth and appreciation of this asset that is so much more expensive than you could afford if you had to buy it outright.
5. So, you can see why the super rich love real estate. Don't you think you should follow their lead in any small way that you can?

Exercises for Keeping Your Investing Blissful

If you would like to use real estate to grow your wealth, and don't want all the stress usually associated with real estate investing, use this simple technique to consistently keep yourself blissful. Here is the technique.

Stop, Drop, Breathe.

- Whenever you are in a stressful situation, are angry, upset, having a hard time with a person, or are trying to make a challenging decision, use this technique.
- Stop: Stress is often caused by all the things that are going on in your head when you are in a challenging situation. So, the first step is to interrupt whatever those thoughts are. So STOP! I say my name to catch my own attention.
- Drop: Into your body and heart. Allow all those clenched muscles to relax. If you can, shake it out a bit.
- Breathe: Now breathe into your heart and feel your body relax further.
- Now deal with your situation from this place of being relaxed and compassionate. You'll make better decisions, build better relationships, and feel much more blissful.

Step 14
How to Get Started Now

Here are the steps you need to get started building your real estate fortune now:

1. Determine your goals.
2. Determine your strategy.
3. Find a mortgage broker.
4. Arrange financing.
5. Determine which areas you would like to invest in.
6. Find a realtor that specializes in those areas.
7. Search for properties.
8. Look at properties.
9. Make offers.
10. Once an offer gets accepted, go through closing process.
11. Prepare property for rent.
12. Seek tenants for the property.
13. Train Tenants.
14. Rent out property.
15. Rinse and Repeat. :D

Exercise to Get Started Investing in Real Estate

You now have everything you need to get started on your journey towards becoming a real estate investor. But remember, nothing happens until you take action.

Start taking actions today:

- If you haven't already, finish the exercises in steps 2, 3, and 4 to determine your goals.
- Complete the exercise in step 5 to determine what strategy you'd like to pursue in real estate.
- Find a mortgage broker and get your financing set up so you know how much you can afford to buy.

Do these three things in the next month. You will have your momentum going to take the next steps in the following month.

Set a monthly goal for yourself and go after each one.

Your consistent action will lead you toward your success, wealth, and blissful life.

Step 15
What Are You Waiting For?

In this Itty Bitty Book I've given you all the steps you need to get started investing in real estate. Have you started taking action?

If not, why not? There may be several reasons.

1. **You've decided this isn't for you**. If this is you, consider why you picked this book up in the first place. What is it that you were hoping to learn or achieve? Can you achieve that goal in another way? If so, take action on that. If not, dig deeper as to why you don't want to move forward investing in real estate.
2. **You still don't know how to get started.** It may feel like you don't know enough by reading such a short book. Real estate investing seems so complicated, is this really all you need to know? I understand where you're coming from. Remember, don't over-complicate things. Real Estate can be very simple. This book shows you how.
3. **You're afraid you are going to make a mistake.** I have suffered from this fear my whole life. And yes, I do make mistakes. But if you're not willing to make mistakes, you will never take action and you will never be successful.

The Solution to Not Being Able to Take Action.

There is a solution for all of the above issues you may be experiencing. That is to get a mentor. A mentor can help you in several ways.

- They have the experience you don't have and can help you avoid many mistakes.
- They can save you a lot of money and heartache by avoiding those mistakes.
- They can keep you accountable so you actually do take action. Did you know that it has been proven that if you have an accountability coach you are 76% more likely to achieve your goals than if you try to do it alone?

I'd love the opportunity to be considered to be your investing mentor. To find out more about me you can…

- Listen to my podcast on Apple called Real Estate Investing for Women.
- You can download my free report explaining the specific strategy I used to turn $10,000 into over $2,000,000 at www.blissfulinvestor.com.
- You can look me up on YouTube and see my many videos about my strategy and philosophy.
- Join me for open discussion on my Facebook group called Blissful Real Estate Investor at https://www.facebook.com/groups/blissfulinvestor/

I would love the opportunity to work with you and look forward to hearing from you soon.

You've finished. Before you go…

<u>Tweet/share that you finished this book.</u>

Please star rate this book on Amazon.

Reviews are solid gold to writers. Please take a few minutes to give us some itty bitty feedback on this book.

ABOUT THE AUTHOR

Moneeka Sawyer is often described as one of the most blissful people you will ever meet. She has been investing in Real Estate for over 25 years, so has been through all the different cycles of the market. Still, she has turned $10,000 into over $2,000,000, working only 5-10 hours per MONTH with very little stress.

While building her multi-million dollar business, she has travelled to over 55 countries, dances every single day, and spends lots of time with her husband of over 25 years and her adorable little puppy (who is the love of her life, but shhhh...don't tell her husband).

Sawyer is the best-selling author of the award-winning book "Choose Bliss: The Power and Practice of Joy and Contentment."

She is also the host of the Podcast Real Estate Investing for Women and her expertise, and bliss-filled laugh, have been featured internationally on stages, radio, podcasts and TV stations including ABC, CBS, FOX, and the CW, reaching over 100 million people.

Itty Bitty Books

If you liked this book you might also enjoy...

- **Your Amazing Itty Bitty® Sell Your Home Book** – Eduardo Mendoza

- **Your Amazing Itty Bitty® Real Estate Exam Book** – Stephanie Stern

- **Your Amazing Itty Bitty® Tax Assessment Prevention Book** – Nellie Williams, EA

....and many more Itty Bitty® Books available on line.

Non-Fiction by Moneeka Sawyer

- Choose Bliss: The Power and Practice of Joy and Contentment

- Discover Your Inspiration Moneeka Sawyer Edition: Real Stories by Real People to Inspire and Ignite Your Soul